A TRUE BOOK™

T0191339

THE EARTH AT RISK

OCEANS IN DANGER

Alicia Green

Children's Press®
An imprint of Scholastic Inc.

Content Consultant
Sara E. Cannon, Ph.D.
Centre for Indigenous Fisheries
Institute for the Oceans and Fisheries
University of British Columbia

Library of Congress Cataloging-in-Publication Data available
ISBN 978-1-5461-0203-8 (library binding) | ISBN 978-1-5461-0204-5 (paperback) |
ISBN 978-1-5461-0205-2 (ebook)

10 9 8 7 6 5 4 3 2 1   25 26 27 28 29

Printed in China 62
First edition, 2025

Design by Kathleen Petelinsek
Series produced by Spooky Cheetah Press

Front cover: Today, the ocean biome is facing several threats, such as pollution, overfishing, and rising temperatures.

Find the Truth!

Everything you are about to read is true *except* for one of the sentences on this page.

Which one is **TRUE**?

T or F Coral reefs are made of colorful rocks.

T or F The oceans are heating up faster than ever before.

Find the answers in this book.

What's in This Book?

Many animals live in and among coral reefs.

4

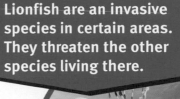

Lionfish are an invasive species in certain areas. They threaten the other species living there.

The BIG Truth

Islands of Garbage

Sea lions are found in coastal areas around the world.

When you see a photo of Earth from space, you'll notice our planet is mostly blue. That's because the **ocean covers about 70 percent** of Earth's surface. This large body of **salt water** is the largest **biome** in the world. There are many **ecosystems** within the ocean, including coral reefs.

There is enough salt in the ocean to cover the surface of Earth. It would form a layer as thick as a 40-story building is tall!

Hundreds of thousands of different **plants** and animals live in the world's ocean. Sadly, this biome, and creatures that live in it, are **under threat** from human activity. Luckily, people around the world are working to save these wild places.

Earth is often referred to as "the Blue Planet."

Ocean Regions and Coral Reefs Around the World

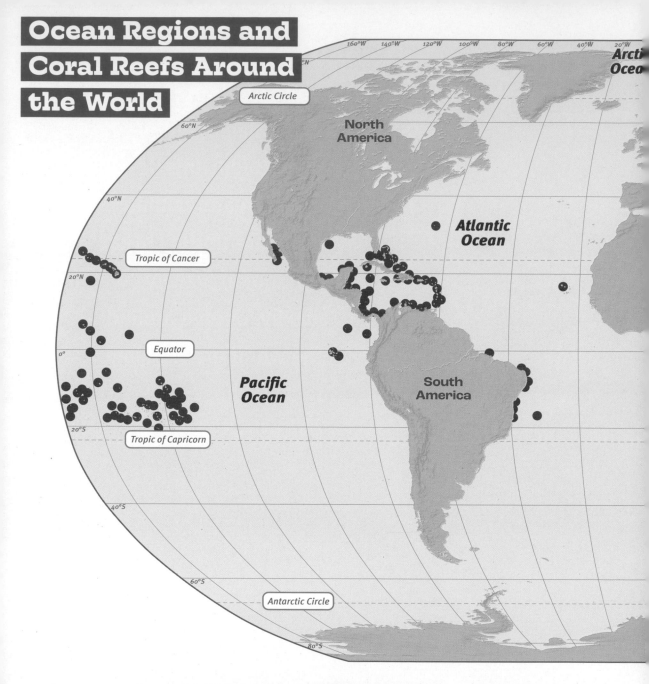

There is only **one world ocean**. Because the ocean is so large, it is broken up into **five named regions**, as well as many smaller seas.

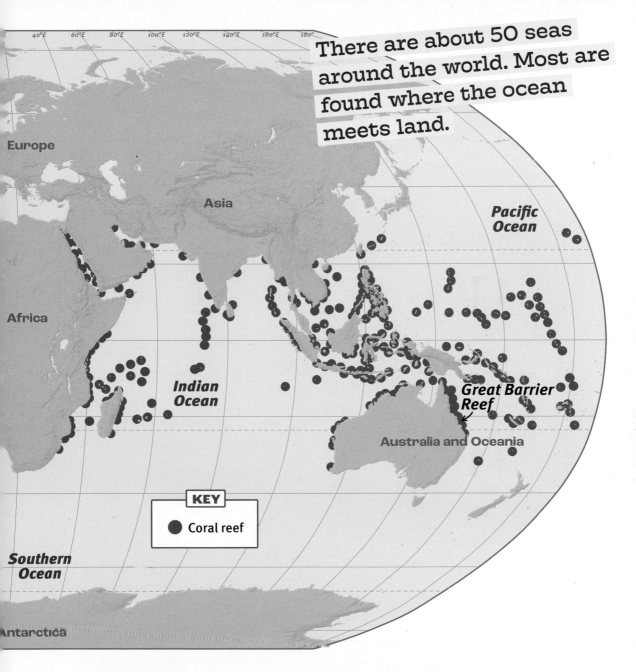

There are about 50 seas around the world. Most are found where the ocean meets land.

40°E 60°E 80°E 100°E 120°E 140°E 160°E 180°

Europe

Asia

Pacific Ocean

Africa

Indian Ocean

Great Barrier Reef

Australia and Oceania

Southern Ocean

Antarctica

KEY

● Coral reef

Coral reefs can be found in the **Atlantic**, **Indian**, and **Pacific Oceans**. Most occur between the Tropic of Cancer and the Tropic of Capricorn.

About 90 percent of the ocean remains unexplored. Approximately 240,000 ocean species have been described— which is just a fraction of the total.

Blue whales are found in every ocean except the Arctic.

Life in the Ocean

Many plant and animal species are found in the ocean. You'll find the planet's smallest creatures there, as well as the largest. Zooplankton are tiny free-floating organisms that you need a microscope to see. The blue whale is a marine mammal that can grow up to 110 feet (33.5 meters) and weigh as much as 400,000 pounds (181,436.9 kilograms). That's about the weight of 16 school buses. The ocean is made up of five different zones. The water gets darker and colder the deeper you go.

zooplankton

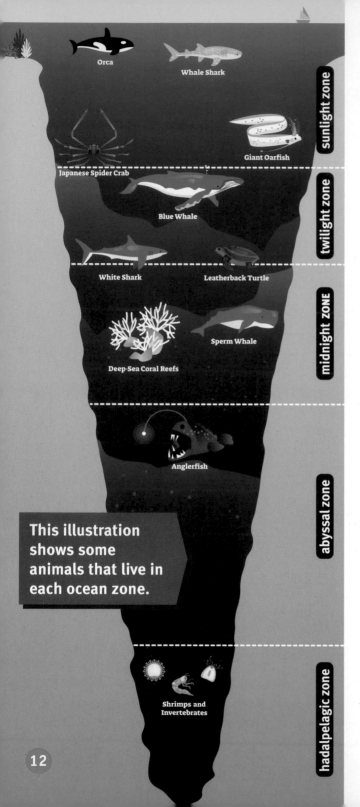

Orca

Whale Shark

Giant Oarfish

Japanese Spider Crab

Blue Whale

White Shark

Leatherback Turtle

Sperm Whale

Deep-Sea Coral Reefs

Anglerfish

This illustration shows some animals that live in each ocean zone.

Shrimps and Invertebrates

The Ocean's Zones

The sunlight zone starts at the ocean's surface. It is the sunniest and warmest zone. Many plants and animals live there. The twilight zone gets a little sunlight. No plants can live in this cold zone, but some animals do. The hadalpelagic zone is the coldest, darkest, and deepest ocean zone. Fewer animals live there than in the rest of the ocean.

seagrass

giant kelp

About half of the oxygen in our atmosphere comes from ocean plants and algae.

red algae

phytoplankton

Green and Growing

Many plants and **algae** are found in the sunlight zone. They provide food and shelter for a wide variety of animals. Seagrass is a common marine plant. Kelp, red algae, and phytoplankton are all types of algae. Algae don't have roots or stems, so they are not plants. But, like plants, algae undergo **photosynthesis**.

Super Swimmers

Marine mammals such as whales, dolphins, and sea lions live in the ocean. They have lungs and must rise to the surface to breathe air. Plenty of fish species live in the ocean too, including sharks. Whale sharks are the largest fish in the world. Most fish have gills to breathe underwater. Many fish live in large groups called schools.

dolphin

sea lion

whale shark

school of yellow-ribbon sweetlips

More than 500 species of sharks are found in the ocean. Some are very large. Others are only the length of a person's hand.

Where Oceans Meet Rivers

An **estuary** is an ecosystem where a river meets the ocean. The oyster is one of very few animals that stay in estuaries their whole lives. Most species, including sea otters and seals, move between estuaries and the ocean. Some, like sea bass, come to estuaries only to reproduce. When their offspring grow up, they return to the ocean.

Estuaries are called "nurseries of the sea" because many animals reproduce there.

oysters

sea otters

sea bass

The Wells National Estuarine Research Reserve is in Maine in the United States.

More than One Home

Many creatures are found in several parts of the ocean. For example, jellyfish are often found near the water's surface and sea stars live in warm, tropical waters. Both species also live in the cold hadalpelagic zone. Some crabs, shrimp, and lobsters live close to shore, and others are also found at the bottom of the ocean.

jellyfish

sea stars

shrimp

snow crab

More than 10 billion snow crabs disappeared in 2022. Scientists believe that happened because the ocean is warming.

The deepest spot in the ocean is found in the Mariana Trench. It is 6.8 miles (11 kilometers) below the surface.

comb jelly

anglerfish

When light from a camera hits a comb jelly, its combs give off a pattern of shifting colors.

Adapted to the Deep

Animals that live in the cold, dark zones of the ocean (the midnight, abyssal, and hadalpelagic zones) have **adaptations** that help them survive. The anglerfish has a glowing lure that helps it attract prey. Comb jellies are transparent. They blend in with their environment, making it hard for **predators** to find them.

This coral reef is in the Andaman Sea near Thailand.

Some corals can live for 4,000 years.

CHAPTER

2

All About Coral Reefs

Coral reefs are marine ecosystems that cover about one percent of the ocean floor and provide a habitat for almost one-quarter of all ocean species. You might think these structures are made of stone. However, they are made up of animals called coral polyps. Polyps have soft bodies and create limestone skeletons for support. When a large number of polyps come together, they build on one another to create coral reefs.

Reef Plants

There are usually few plants in a coral reef ecosystem. That is partly because the ecosystem is built from corals themselves. There is often not enough space for plants to grow. One type of algae is crucial to corals, though: zooxanthellae. Coral polyps get most of their nutrients from these tiny algae, which live in the polyps' tissues.

Coral polyps are see-through. They get their color from zooxanthellae.

corals

stingray

sponge

dugong

sea snail

Life in the Reef

Plenty of animals live in and around coral reefs, including crabs, stingrays, and sponges. Marine mammals like dugongs and brightly colored fish are found there too. Some animals that live in coral reefs are hard to see. For example, sea snails, slugs, and tiny fish can hide from predators in a reef's nooks and crannies.

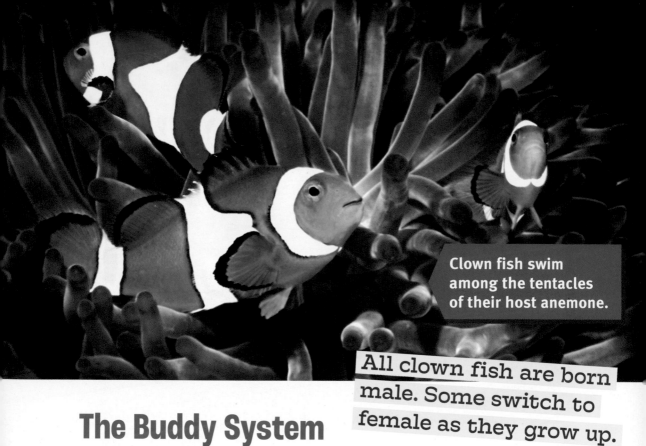

Clown fish swim among the tentacles of their host anemone.

All clown fish are born male. Some switch to female as they grow up.

The Buddy System

Clown fish are some of the best-known reef dwellers. They have a special relationship with sea anemones—stinging animals that are related to corals. Clown fish are covered in a layer of mucus that protects them from an anemone's sting. They live among the anemone's tentacles to stay safe from predators. In return, the anemone gets to feed on scraps left over from the clown fish's meals.

World's Greatest Reef

The Great Barrier Reef, which is located off the northeast coast of Australia, is the world's largest coral reef system. In fact, it is visible from outer space! The reef stretches 1,429 mi. (2,299.7 km).

About 9,000 species of plants and animals live in the Great Barrier Reef, including the manta ray. This interesting fish, which is related to sharks, can grow to up to 29 ft. (8.8 m) long!

manta ray

About 10 percent of all fish species on Earth can be found within the Great Barrier Reef system.

Islands of Garbage

In the middle of the Pacific Ocean, between Asia and North America, there are two huge collections of marine debris made up of discarded fishing gear and tiny floating pieces of plastic. Together they are known as the Great Pacific Garbage Patch (GPGP). Even though the GPGP is made up of litter that ends up in the ocean, it has somehow become its own ocean ecosystem. Discover more about the Great Pacific Garbage Patch—and how it's affecting marine life.

HOW DID IT FORM?

The ocean has many currents. A current is the movement of water in a certain direction. Gyres are large systems of ocean currents. They pull debris into one spot. The GPGP was slowly formed as the Pacific Gyre gathered large amounts of marine debris in one spot.

gyre seen from space

microplastics

HOW BIG IS IT?

The GPGP shifts with the wind and currents, so its size is always changing. Even if there is no exact measurement, we know it's big—more than twice the size of Texas! There are an estimated 1.8 trillion pieces of plastic in the patch, and that number grows every day. Microplastics that are no bigger than a sesame seed account for 94 percent of that plastic.

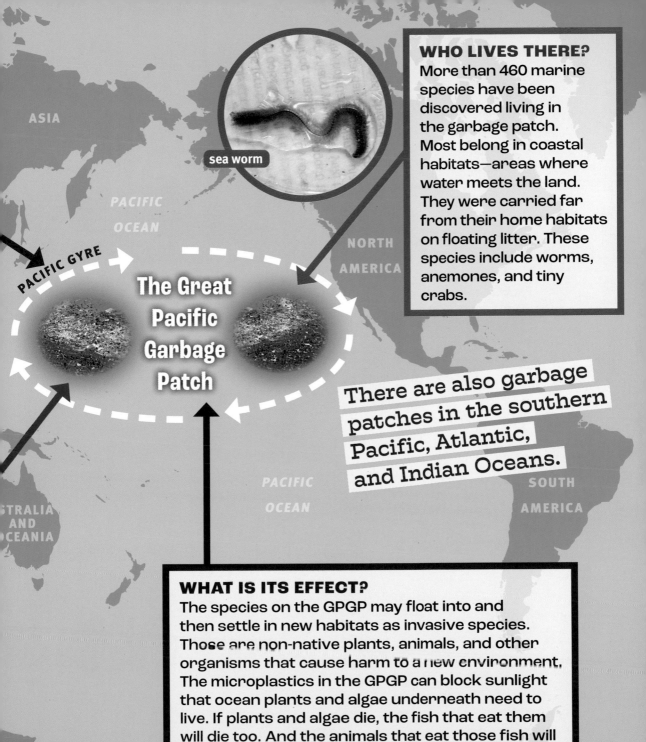

ASIA

PACIFIC
OCEAN

sea worm

PACIFIC GYRE

The Great
Pacific
Garbage
Patch

NORTH
AMERICA

PACIFIC
OCEAN

SOUTH
AMERICA

STRALIA
AND
CEANIA

NTARCTICA

WHO LIVES THERE?
More than 460 marine species have been discovered living in the garbage patch. Most belong in coastal habitats—areas where water meets the land. They were carried far from their home habitats on floating litter. These species include worms, anemones, and tiny crabs.

There are also garbage patches in the southern Pacific, Atlantic, and Indian Oceans.

WHAT IS ITS EFFECT?
The species on the GPGP may float into and then settle in new habitats as invasive species. Those are non-native plants, animals, and other organisms that cause harm to a new environment. The microplastics in the GPGP can block sunlight that ocean plants and algae underneath need to live. If plants and algae die, the fish that eat them will die too. And the animals that eat those fish will suffer as well. It affects the entire **food chain**.

25

Discarded clothing covers this beach on the coast of Ghana, a country in Africa.

It is estimated that 25 percent of all ocean mammals are **endangered**. That means they are at risk of becoming extinct.

Oceans Under Threat

Climate change is what we call the changes in the weather and weather patterns that are happening on Earth because of human activity. One of these changes is **global warming**, the gradual rise in the temperature of Earth's atmosphere. Climate change is causing problems across every biome on the planet. In the ocean, it has caused water temperatures to rise. Climate change, pollution, overfishing, and invasive species are all big threats to our fragile ocean biome and all the animals that live in it.

Climate Control

Normally the ocean can absorb heat without its temperature greatly increasing. That is how the ocean helps regulate our planet's climate. Now, however, global warming has caused Earth's surface temperature to rise faster than normal. The ocean has absorbed more than 90 percent of that extra heat. That has caused the ocean to heat up too.

Marine heatwaves are long periods where the ocean is hotter than usual.

Polar bears lose important hunting grounds when rising temperatures cause sea ice to melt.

This photo shows corals before (left) and after (right) bleaching.

Problems for Corals

When the ocean gets too warm, corals become stressed and remove the zooxanthellae living in their tissues. That is called bleaching. It makes corals turn completely white. Zooxanthellae don't just provide color to corals. They also provide food. Most corals can't live without them for long. When corals die, entire reef ecosystems are affected.

Marine animals are disappearing from their habitats faster than land animals.

This sperm whale washed up on a beach in Indonesia.

Too Hot

Rising temperatures can cause food shortages too. For example, plankton, including zooplankton and phytoplankton, are very sensitive to changes in temperature. These tiny organisms are at the bottom of the marine food chain. If the plankton die, animals farther up the food chain will have less food to eat.

Too Fast

Rising temperatures also make ocean currents move faster. Currents carry animals and food through the ocean. Some zooplankton (like fish larvae) become stronger swimmers as they grow larger, which allows them to exit or swim against the currents. But they may not be strong enough to do that when the currents are faster than what they are used to. As a result, they may get pushed into new habitats.

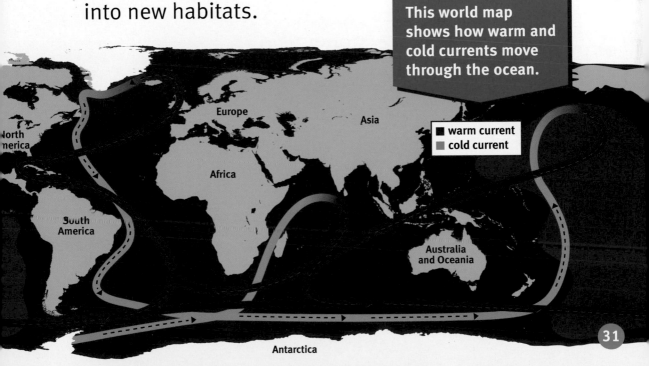

This world map shows how warm and cold currents move through the ocean.

■ warm current
■ cold current

Europe

Asia

North America

Africa

South America

Australia and Oceania

Antarctica

Too High

Ocean water expands as it warms. This has added to rising sea levels around the globe. Warming temperatures cause ice sheets and glaciers to melt, which also causes sea levels to rise. A rise in sea levels can destroy coastal cities and animal habitats, such as beaches. Animals like the Hawaiian monk seal rely on beaches as nursery grounds.

By 2050, sea levels are expected to rise by 12 inches (30 centimeters).

monk seals

Rising waters overtook these homes in Florida.

This seal is caught in a fishing net.

A plastic bag might look like a jellyfish to a hungry sea turtle.

Scientists say there will be more plastic in the ocean than fish by 2050.

Oceans of Trash

Every year, billions of pounds of trash and other pollution enter the ocean. Many animals are affected by ocean garbage. For example, turtles mistake plastic for food. They can choke on it and die. Animals can also get trapped in plastic bags and fishing gear. They may be injured or drown.

Too Much Fishing

Overfishing is when humans take too many fish from the ocean to sell and eat. Fish are captured faster than their populations can recover. This can wipe out entire fish species. Wiping out a species of fish can often mean wiping out another animal's food source, which can harm entire ecosystems.

IT2-5001

Nets make it possible to catch hundreds of fish at once.

A single lionfish can eat more than 5,000 fish in one year!

Lionfish are native to the Pacific Ocean. They have flourished in the Atlantic after being introduced in the 1990s.

Invasive Species

As you've read, invasive species can enter an ecosystem via trash pollution. They are also carried by currents and cargo ships. Sometimes they come from people dumping their aquarium fish into waterways. Invasive species compete with native species for resources. They may spread diseases or even prey on native species.

Protecting Marine Animals

There are important laws in place to help save marine habitats and species. Marine protected areas (MPAs) are one example. These **sanctuaries** are parts of the ocean where a government limits human activity. Some MPAs ban people from fishing but allow them to use the area for swimming or snorkeling.

About eight percent of the world's ocean is protected by MPAs.

Tourists at this Bahamas MPA are observing sharks from a cage.

These Adélie penguins live in the Ross Sea region.

PACIFIC OCEAN

SOUTHERN OCEAN

Ross Sea

Protected zone →

ANTARCTICA

INDIAN OCEAN

SOUTHERN OCEAN

ATLANTIC OCEAN

The Ross Sea region is about 1.5 times the size of Northeast Greenland National Park—the largest national park on land.

The Last Ocean

The Ross Sea region is in the Southern Ocean near Antarctica. It is the world's largest marine protected area. It is nicknamed "The Last Ocean." That's because it is the only part of the ocean that has been mostly untouched by humans—though it is still affected by climate change. The Ross Sea is home to a variety of penguins, seals, whales, seabirds, and fish.

Going to the Nursery

Coral nurseries are another way experts are protecting these ecosystems. A coral nursery is a place on land or in water where new corals are grown. The new corals may be started by baby corals or pieces of corals that have been rescued from the ocean floor. The corals are cared for until they can be replanted on damaged reefs.

Timeline: Oceans Under Threat

3.8 BILLION YEARS AGO
The world ocean forms.

252 MILLION YEARS AGO
Approximately 96 percent of all marine species go extinct during "The Great Dying."

1998
The ocean has its first modern global mass coral bleaching event. About eight percent of the world's corals are killed.

Our Ocean's Future

You've taken the first step toward protecting our planet's ocean just by reading this book. Now share what you've learned with others. The more people know about this biome, the more likely they will be to protect it. If we act now to stop these threats, marine life could recover by 2050. We can make a change if we all work together!

2023
Ocean surface temperatures hit a modern record high around the world.

2050
Most of the world's coral reefs are likely to die off due to ocean warming if we don't act fast enough.

2100
If climate change continues, 90 percent of marine species could face extinction.

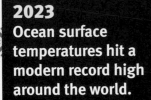

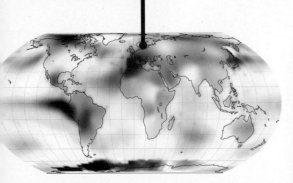

39

Amazing Comeback

Humpback whales live in every ocean around the world. It is believed that, at one time, there may have been as many as 125,000 humpbacks living in Earth's waters. Then, over time, humpback whales disappeared from the ocean due to commercial whaling. People hunted the whales to sell their meat for food and their blubber for oil. By the 1970s, the number of humpback whales left alive was thought to be around 10,000.

A turning point came when the humpback whale was one of the first animals to be protected under the Endangered Species Conservation Act. In the United States, humpbacks were also protected under the Marine Mammal Protection Act. Those laws, and an international ban on whaling, helped increase humpback numbers around the globe. Today, experts believe there are as many as 80,000 humpbacks swimming in our oceans.

Kid Heroes

Madison Checketts, from Eagle Mountain, Utah, is passionate about helping to end plastic pollution. In fact, she is so passionate about getting rid of plastic that she invented an edible water bottle when she was 12 years old! The Eco-Hero looks like a water balloon and holds about ¾ cup of water (175 milliliters). To drink from it, a person bites a hole in the bottle, then squeezes the water into their mouth. Once the water is gone, the person can eat the bottle. Here, Madison tells us a bit about her journey to creating this amazing invention.

1

Q: What inspired you to create the Eco-Hero?

A: I wanted to make a difference in the world, even if it was small. When I went to the beach in California, I noticed there were plastic water bottles in the sand. I wondered if there was a way to make a water bottle that wasn't made of plastic so it wouldn't pollute.

2

Q: What materials did you use to make the Eco-Hero?

A: I tested different safe-to-eat materials using different amounts of each until I found the right combination. A combination of calcium lactate, xanthan gum, lemon juice, and water made the water bottle strong enough to hold water without breaking in my hand.

Eco-Hero

3

Q: What are your plans for the Eco-Hero?

A: I want to make it stronger and bigger so it holds more water. I would love to find a way to make it resealable. That way people could use it more than once. My goal is to have people use it to reduce plastic usage and help our oceans and our environment be cleaner.

4

Q: Why is this issue important to you?

A: It is important for animals and plants in the ocean to be able to live and continue to grow. The ocean is important to humans too. We need to keep our ocean clean so future generations can enjoy and benefit from everything it provides to us.

True Statistics*

Total number of named ocean regions: 5

Percentage of Earth that is covered by ocean: About 70%

Average depth of the Pacific Ocean: 14,040 feet (4,280 m)

Number of identified ocean plant and animal species: 240,000—more than 2,000 of which are endangered or threatened

Percentage of marine animals that rely on coral reefs: 25%

Length of the Great Barrier Reef: 1,429 miles (2,299.7 km)

Amount of plastic in the Great Pacific Garbage Patch: About 1.8 trillion pieces

Percentage of Earth's excess heat the ocean absorbs: 90%

*As of 2024

Did you find the truth?

F Coral reefs are made of colorful rocks.

T The oceans are heating up faster than ever before.

Resources

Other books in this series:

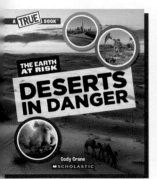   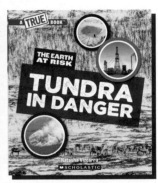

You can also look at:

Free, Katie. *Animals in Danger*. NY: Scholastic, 2020.

Hestermann, Beth, and Josh Hestermann. *The Fascinating Ocean Book for Kids*. Emeryville, CA: Rockridge Press, 2021.

Macdonald, Fiona. *The Science of Oceans*. NY: Scholastic, 2018.

Spencer, Erin. *The World of Coral Reefs*. North Adams, MA: Storey Publishing, 2022.

Wilsdon, Christina. *Ultimate Oceanpedia: The Most Complete Ocean Reference Ever*. Washington, DC: National Geographic Kids, 2016.

Glossary

adaptations (ad-ap-TAY-shuhnz) changes that a living thing goes through so it fits in better with its environment

algae (AL-jee) small plants without roots or stems that grow mainly in water

biome (BYE-ohm) a region of the world with similar animals and plants

ecosystems (EE-koh-sis-tuhmz) all the living things in a place and their relation to their environment

endangered (en-DAYN-jurd) in danger of becoming extinct, usually because of human activity

estuary (ES-choo-er-ee) the wide part of a river, where it joins the ocean

food web (FOOD WEB) an arrangement of animals and plants in which each feeds on the one below it in the chain

global warming (GLOH-buhl WOR-ming) a gradual rise in the temperature of Earth's atmosphere, caused by human activities that pollute

photosynthesis (foh-toh-SIN-thi-sis) a chemical process by which plants and some other organisms make their food

predators (PRED-uh-turz) animals that live by hunting other animals for food

sanctuaries (SANGK-choo-er-eez) natural areas where birds or animals are protected from hunters

Index

Page numbers in **bold** indicate illustrations.

About the Author

Alicia Green is a journalist with a passion for storytelling. Her stories reach third- to sixth-grade students across the United States. She enjoys writing articles that intrigue children and teach them something new. Her goal is to help educate kids in fun and unique ways. *Oceans in Danger* is Alicia's third True Book.

Photos ©: cover background: M.M. Sweet/Getty Images; cover top left: Brett Monroe Garner/Getty Images; cover bottom: Rosemary Calvert/Getty Images; back cover: Jodi Jacobson/Getty Images; 3: Mike Hill/Getty Images; 4: VitalyEdush/Getty Images; 5 bottom: Philip Thurston/Getty Images; 8–9: Jim McMahon/Mapman ®; 10–11 main: Phillip Colla/Blue Planet Archive; 11 inset: Roland Birke/Getty Images; 13 top right: Douglas Klug/Getty Images; 13 bottom right: Stephanie Anderson/University of Rhode Island/NASA; 14 top left: Mike Hill/Getty Images; 14 top center: Philip Thurston/Getty Images; 14 top right: crisod/Getty Images; 14 bottom: MartinHristov/Getty Images; 15 background: Ultima_Gaina/Getty Images; 15 center inset: Temujin Nana/Getty Images; 15 bottom inset: Reinhard Dirscherl/Getty Images; 16 top left: vojce/Getty Images; 16 top right: Damocean/Getty Images; 16 bottom left: Bruce Patten/Dreamstime; 17 main: Theodore W Pietsch/Univ Wash/Shutterstock; 18–19: Georgette Douwma/Getty Images; 20: VitalyEdush/Getty Images; 21 bottom left: cinoby/Getty Images; 21 bottom right: Brandon Rosenblum/Getty Images; 22: Jodi Jacobson/Getty Images; 23 inset: Aaron Bull/Getty Images; 24 top inset: SeaWiFS Project/NASA/Goddard Space Flight Center/ORBIMAGE; 25 center: Juan Camilo Bernal/Getty Images; 26–27: Muntaka Chasant/Shutterstock; 28: Patricia Hamilton/Getty Images; 29 all: Richard Vevers/Ocean Image Bank; 30: Riza Azhari/Getty Images; 32 main: Aerial_Views/Getty Images; 32 inset: MediaPunch/Shutterstock; 33 right: Paul A. Souders/Getty Images; 34: Ryouchin/Getty Images; 36: Stephen Frink/Getty Images; 37 main: Kevin Schafer/Getty Images; 37 inset: The Design Lab; 38 right: Richard Vevers/Ocean Image Bank; 39 left: Lauren Dauphin/NASA's Earth Observatory; 39 right: Riza Azhari/Getty Images; 40–43 background: billnoll/Getty Images; 43 foreground all: Courtesy Checketts Family; 44: VitalyEdush/Getty Images; 48: Nkosi Hamilton Photography.

All other photos © Shutterstock.